Talking

How to Become
Connect with the Afterlife

Emily Stroia

"Death is no more than passing from one room into another."
— Helen Keller

Copyright © 2015 by Emily Stroia

All rights reserved.

Foreword

Before I discovered the true nature of my abilities as a psychic medium, I had no knowledge of what a medium was or how spirit communication happened. My knowledge of this esoteric world was based off of Hollywood Movies and sidewalk fortune tellers.

As I learned more about mediumship in my training and classes I realized this was an entire world that I had no clue about. It amazed me and blew my mind. I also realized how many misconceptions and ideas there are to mediums and spirits in general.

I wrote this book to share the knowledge I learned in my studies and in my practice as a professional medium. I believe it's important we all know and understand the world of Spirit Communication.

With this book, I hope to explain topics about the Spirit World that will help you better understand their world and ours. I hope after you read this book you too will discover and become more aware, knowledgeable and open to the world that lives beside us. Spirit is always there guiding us on our journey.

Introduction

This book will help you discover and understand the world of Spirit Communication. If you have ever been curious about how to talk to the dead, how they talk to us or communicate with a Spirit Guide, then this is the book for you.

What you will learn in this book:

1. Signs You May be a Medium
2. The Different Types of Mediumship
3. Common Signs & Impressions from Spirits
4. How to Sense Spirit
5. The Purpose of Spirit Guides & How to Meet Yours
6. Mediumship Exercises and more...!

Why develop your mediumistic ability?

1. Personal reasons: Learn how to become aware of your mediumistic ability & develop spiritually
2. Connect with passed loved ones & Spirit Guides
3. Be open to receiving and understanding guidance from the other side
4. Faith in a higher power or universal consciousness
5. Know that physical death isn't the end & that the soul lives on

Spirit communication is a fascinating process and an incredible journey to embark on. If you don't want to be a medium at least you will better know and understand the world of Spirit. You may be able to sense a Spirit in the future or communicate with a passed loved one in your meditation or dream state. There are endless possibilities and uses to Spirit Communication.

Table of Contents

Chapter 1: Why Connect With Spirit?........1

Chapter 2: How Do You Know If You are a Medium?....................................4

Chapter 3: What is Mediumship?..............9

Chapter 4: Types of Mediumship………..14

Chapter 5: What Makes Mediumship Successful..17

Chapter 6: Creating Your Spiritual Toolbox Kit…23

Chapter 7: Sensing Spirit…………………………28

Chapter 8: Recognizing How Spirits Communicate..33

Chapter 9: Common Signs from Spirit……………..35

Chapter 10: Setting Your Intention & Protection…..42

Chapter 11: What's Your Type?...............................46

Chapter 12: Sitting with Spirit & Making Contact…48

Chapter 13: Talking to Spirit……………………….53

Chapter 14: Telling the Story of Your Spirit Loved One……………………………………………….57

Chapter 15: How to Interpret Symbols From Spirit..66

Chapter 16: Spirit Guides & How to Meet Yours….73

Chapter 17: Automatic Writing & Trance Channeling…………………………………….78

Chapter 18: The Afterlife...............................82

Chapter 19: Messages....................................85

Additional Mediumship Exercises......................89

About Emily..93

Chapter 1: Why Connect with Spirit or Practice Mediumship?

When a loved one leaves the Earth and moves on to the Spirit World, we are often left wondering if the person is still around or can communicate with us. Many people have experienced some type of mediumistic phenomena meaning they have felt, seen or communicated with a deceased loved one. I've met clients who have told me they had vivid dreams about their passed loved one or woke up and saw them physically in the room.

There are tons of stories like this and you don't have to be a practicing medium to experience Spirit phenomena or communicate with the afterlife. Before I truly realized my mediumistic ability, I personally thought a person needed to be a medium before trying to connect with passed loved ones or feel any type of Spirit presence. I later realized that it happens when you are open or receptive to that experience.

People also have mediumistic experiences when a loved one passes away and they shared a connection or were influenced by that person. If you have a heart-heart connection with a close relative or partner and he/she passed away it is common to still feel their presence around.

Whether you are a curious reader, intuitive, healer or practicing medium take a moment to ask yourself "Why do I want to connect with passed loved ones?

Why do I want to practice mediumship?." Here are some common reasons why mediums and spiritual practitioners feel drawn to working with Spirit specifically the deceased.

1. **Healing**- Communication with a passed loved one can help people heal in their grief or provide a sense of comfort knowing their loved one is okay in the Spirit World and around them.
2. **Evidence**- Communication with deceased loved ones can prove that life after death continues in a different form. When a medium provides evidential details of the person once alive through communication this can be especially relieving for those concerned about the afterlife and what happen to us after we die.
3. **Deeper Knowledge**- When we communicate with passed loved ones sometimes we receive deeper knowledge and wisdom about our own lives and the afterlife. In the book *The Afterlife of Billy Fingers* the writer discovers some profound things about the afterlife and what happens to the soul. It's quite a fascinating discovery!
4. **Closure**- Often Spirit communication can give closure on the past, unfinished business or traumas that occurred while the person was alive.

For example, a client of mine lost her abusive ex-boyfriend tragically. When she came in for a session there were a lot of unanswered questions and no closure about what happened. Once we were able to connect with him, he provided a ton of evidence and also apologized for his actions.

A year later she returned to me and said her nightmares of him had stopped and she found new love again. I couldn't have been more grateful and touched by such a powerful session.

5. **Service-** Many mediums when asked why they want to be a medium will answer it's just who they are. It's so true! Spirit chooses you for a reason and it's a process to let go and trust that there is another world with us all the time. Once you embrace the call to be a medium you embark on a phenomenal journey of true magic, healing and wisdom. It is your service to the world and to human consciousness.

Chapter 2: How Do You Know if You Are a Medium?

I believe we are all born with a sense of intuition and ability to feel the Spirit World. If we are open and willing I feel that we can sense and communicate with Spirit.

Perhaps you are curious about spirit communication and how to feel them. Or maybe you have sensed Spirit but never actually knew it was someone communicating with you.

I think some of us have paranormal experiences at a young age where others don't have any at all until older. It's all about timing and where we are on our journeys that enable or disable us to feel or speak to Spirits.

How do you know if you are a medium?

A medium is simply one who can sense and communicate with the Spirit World whether it is a passed loved one or a Spirit Guide.

Common Signs You May be a Medium

1. **Childhood Phenomena**- You have memories of seeing or feeling a Spirit around as a child. You may have communicated with deceased relatives or seen them physically in your environment. You may have also had vivid

dreams of a Spirit Friend or deceased loved one.
2. **Natural curiosity**- You may have always had an innate curiosity to Spirituality or felt drawn to psychics, tarot card readers, mediums or other types of spiritual practitioners. Meditation, metaphysical books or bookstores, yoga and any other type of holistic knowledge may peak your interest.
3. **Family History**- You have family members or great relatives who were known to be spiritual healers, psychics or mediums. You may also have close relatives who are also drawn to mysticism or spiritual development and this influence may be in your lineage and genealogy. A family member may have sensed or felt Spirits around
4. **Highly Sensitive & Empathic**- You are a highly sensitive or empathic person and it has always been difficult for you to turn it off. Highly sensitive people (HSP) or empaths are naturally aware of others' emotions and mental states without a lot of prior knowledge of the person. You may pick up on the energy of a place, person or object very quickly and intuitively know that something bad or good happened.
5. **Connected to Nature & Creative Arts**- If you have felt deeply connected to nature or been a creative person you may be sensitive to connecting with the Spirit World or be more open to communication from them. Creativity

and nature deepens our connection to intuition and imagination which allows us to be more open to other possibilities of experience including Spirit Communication.
6. **Heightened Awareness Post-Trauma**- Another sign of a developing medium is someone who has heightened awareness after a traumatic event or life-changing experience. Some people have had near death experiences and then strongly felt the Spirit World around after. People who have also had great epiphanies during a life change or experienced something traumatic like an accident may also be more highly sensitive, aware and open and therefore closer to feeling the Spirit World.
Strong Premonitions & Intuition- You may be a medium if you have experienced strong premonitions or had a sense of something before it happened only to see it come true. If you have had persistent intuitive feelings, a knowing of information without any logical explanation or prior knowledge you may be a medium. You may also have had a sense that a family member died and then later found out the person passed away at the exact same time you had that feeling.
7. **Spirit Phenomena**- You have seen or sensed a Spirit presence at least once in your life. You may have seen a shadow or figure in your peripheral at some point.
8. **Dream Phenomena**- You or a family member may have communicated with a passed loved

one in your sleep or dream state such as feeling a presence by your bedside or talking with a deceased relative in a dream.

Exercise: Close your eyes for a moment and take a couple of deep breaths to ground yourself. Take a moment to reflect on times in your life when you felt more aware or sensitive. Think of any experiences where you may have felt a sense or intuition about something. What feelings came to mind when this experience happened? Or think back on a time where you thought you felt a Spirit presence around or communicated with a deceased loved one? Write down your experience including any physical sensations, images, symbols or words you felt, saw or heard.

Spirit Communication is helpful for when we want to connect with the deceased or receive guidance from Guides.

My family was always into premonitions, psychic dreams and gut feelings. My father had many Spirit visitations from his Mother after she passed away in his dreams.

Even if you haven't had this type of background it doesn't mean you can't communicate with Spirit. You were drawn to buying this book for a reason. Perhaps the knowledge you learn here will help you towards a path to mediumship and spirit communication.

Perhaps you will realize you had some mediumship ability and never knew it until now. Or maybe this book will simply help you grow on your spiritual journey and open a door to something else.

Chapter 3: What is Mediumship?

Before I began my journey into becoming a medium I didn't understand the definition of mediumship or spirit communication at all.

Growing up I thought of Spirits as ghosts who lingered around on the earth and sometimes haunted people or places. I played with Ouija boards occasionally with friends but never actually saw a ghost or experienced anything close to "paranormal".

My intuition led me to take psychic development classes in my early twenties which naturally opened up my mediumistic gifts. In my training my knowledge of psychics, mediums and Spirits changed completely and I learned the true definition to what mediumship actually is.

So what exactly is mediumship?

Mediumship is when a person or "medium" can connect and communicate with passed loved ones or the deceased. This person serves as a mediator or channel between two worlds, the world of the living and of the deceased.

Mediums who communicate with the dead will usually be able to bring forth evidence or details of the deceased person's life to his/her friends or family to verify their existence on the other side.

You may have seen this type of mediumship on TV with well-known mediums such as John Edwards, James Van Praagh or the Long Island Medium Theresa Caputo.

A medium is not to be confused with a psychic!

In my book *Psychic Development for Beginners: A Practical Guide to Developing Your Intuition & Psychic Gifts* I touch on the difference between a psychic and a medium.

A psychic tunes into the energy of the physical environment such as a building, place/area, object, animal or a person to receive intuitive impressions. A medium receives impressions only from a Spirit through telepathy; mind-to-mind communication.

When developing your mediumship it is important to understand the difference between both a psychic and a medium and what true mediumship is.

We have seen the use of mediums in history in various cultures and environments. In primitive times and tribes a trance/witch doctor or "shaman" would connect with ancestral energies, Nature Spirits and Guides to access divine wisdom and/or heal members of the tribe of illnesses and diseases.

Shamans are still around today and often consulted for similar practices such as holistic healing, and emotional release.

There are other examples of mediumship throughout history such as the Greeks consulting with the Oracles for advice. Also, the Assyrians and Romans practiced divination to obtain guidance from the Gods.

Witches were also believed to be mediums and were killed, tortured and burned to death by "witch-hunters".

Mediumship became more taboo over time and later was resurrected by two sisters known as Margaret & Catherine Fox in 1848. The sisters established communication with a spirit entity in their house through the use of noisy rappings or "knocks" on the walls.

The spirit was trying to communicate a message to the sisters about the location of his body in the house which created a lot of publicity for mediumship and opened the door for modern-day Spiritualism to be practiced again.

Spiritualism became more well-known and widespread throughout America and Great Britain The first Spiritualist church and newspaper was created in Great Britain. Many home circles or séances and spiritualist societies also developed.

A well-known case of Spiritualism in America was Mary Todd Lincoln who grieving the loss of her son organized séances in the White House, also attended by Abraham Lincoln.

Spiritualism was later defined as a "religion". However the only difference between Spiritualism and other common religions was the use of mediums to provide evidence of the afterlife and continuity of the soul's existence.

Today there are Spiritualist churches are all over America and in the Great Britain area. One well-known Spiritualist church is *The Journey Within* in the New Jersey area and also *Lilydale* in upstate New York.

These churches provide Sunday service with an inspirational message delivered by a medium or healer, followed by a healing service and then a mediumship demonstration to the audience. A mediumship demonstration is when a medium stands up in front of an audience and delivers messages from the deceased to their loved ones in the crowd.

Mediums are not able to summon or call up these people as one would phone a friend but rather Spirit chooses to come to the medium when they are ready, willing and able to do so.

Some well-known mediums in history are Estelle Roberts, coined as the "perfect medium", Helen Hughes and Emma Hardinge Britten.

Modern-day mediums of our time are John Holland, James Van Praagh, Colette Baron Reid, Tony Stockwell and Mavis Pittila who continue to bring forth strong mediumship and knowledge in demonstrations, workshops and books.

Chapter 4: Types of Mediumship

There are several types of mediumship in Spirit Communication. Personally, I am an evidential medium but every medium feels drawn to their own style of mediumship. There is no right or wrong path to a style of mediumship.

1. **Evidential Mediumship-** A medium who is able to communicate with passed loved ones/deceased and communicate evidence or details of the person's life when he/she was alive.

    Some examples of evidential details are type of passing, age of passing, when the person died, memories with family or friends, hobbies, names/dates, relationship to the person in the reading, who they are with on the other side such as other deceased family or friends, and more.

2. **Trance Mediumship** – Trance mediumship is when a medium enters a deep trance state either through meditation or hypnosis. These states can vary between light to very deep and achieved with practice over a period of time.

    In this altered state a spirit guide will blend his/her energy with the medium and use the medium's voice as an instrument to communicate. This is also similar to automatic writing where a medium channels information from a guide through handwriting.

3. **Physical Mediumship-** Physical mediumship is a phenomena in which a spirit communicates using physical objects or manifestations through the environment such as temperature changes, knocks or raps on the walls, lights flickering, electricity phenomena via television, radio or cell phone. A spirit may physically appear through physical manifestation.

This type of phenomena usually is caused from high emotion or concentrated focus through meditation. In séance circles, the same group of people would sit once a week for months together and build up the energy to create physical phenomena in the room.

This phenomena would manifest from the medium's face and body through physical materialization into an actual Spirit Guide forming into a nearly solid person for the group to witness through a process called ectoplasm.

Ectoplasm is a plasma-like substance that is formed from the medium's body creating images, faces, and physical matter of a Spirit or Spirits.

4. **Mental Mediumship**- Mental Mediumship is the process of communication with Spirit through mind-to-mind communication or telepathy similar to evidential mediumship, inspirational thought or writing. This type of mediumship also occurs in dreams and with our paraphysical senses such as clairvoyance, clairsentience and clairaudience.

    With mental mediumship, Spirit will impress feelings, images and thoughts telepathically to us throughout the day or in our dream state to communicate a message or send us guidance. It's only when we are open and aware of these impressions do we understand and recognize Spirit is trying to communicate.

Chapter 5: What Makes Mediumship Successful

Contacting Spirit is such a powerful and emotionally moving experience. My first time practicing mediumship I was literally blown away by the signals, subtle feelings, sensations and messages Spirit was trying to give me. I couldn't believe how much information was actually conveyed in the smallest ways.

When you practice mediumship you want to have a method of connecting that works for you. Contacting Spirit isn't like calling up a friend on speed dial and he/she will immediately pick up. As you have read in the other chapters it is a process and takes a little bit of preparation to successfully connect with the Spirit World.

Before making contact with Spirit you first need to know what makes the connection with a Spirit successful.

Exercise: If you were to go to a medium to connect with a passed relative or friend, what are some things you'd like to know if the medium is truly talking to your loved one? Take a moment to think about it and feel free to write it down.

Personally, I'd like the medium to give some details and memories I shared with my passed loved one and if he/she has a message or guidance on my life direction. We all have different reasons for wanting to see a medium but I think these are some common things that really do make Spirit communication and mediumship successful.

1. **Evidence**- You want to be able to communicate evidence or details about the person you are communicating with to your sitter or client. Details include sex, age of passing, how they passed, relationship to the client, memories, hobbies, personality and more if you can as well as a message. Why did the Spirit come to talk to their loved one? What does he/she want to say?
2. **Verification**- Before you go into the story of the Spirit person you're connecting with you always want to make sure the details you are receiving are verified by your client or sitter.

For example, the medium may feel a grandfather figure who was in the military and who died of lung cancer. The sitter must be able to understand these details and verify that he/she knew a grandfather who died of cancer and was in the military. Once this is verified the medium can continue to go into more details and see if there is a message.

You want to be able to verify the details for both the sitter, yourself and the Spirit you are working with. If you aren't able to receive strong verification then it would be best to move on to another Spirit the client can identify better.

Verification is especially important for you as a medium, the sitter and the Spirit communicating. When you receive verification about the information received you will improve your mediumship. This helps you to know what information received accurately and inaccurately and how to interpret it better. Verification also gives the sitter the awareness of his/her Spirit Loved One actually there proving the existence of the afterlife.

3. **Message**- Whenever a spirit contact is made the sitter or client always wants to know what the person wants to say. The Spirit came for a reason so always be sure to ask "What would you like to say to your loved one?" They always come for different reasons. Sometimes they give a message of closure, forgiveness, love or direction. No message is too cliché. The simplest message may mean the world to the client.

For example, a deceased Father may connect with his daughter just to give the message that he's proud of her because he never said it enough when he was alive.

Making Contact

When making contact with Spirit you want to be in a grounded, relaxed and focused state. If your mind is crowded with thoughts or if you are highly anxious you may block the flow of information. You may not be as receptive and feel you aren't receiving much or anything at all.

In my classes I have seen students get so nervous and say they aren't getting anything when they actually are. Once they take a step back, relax and focus they start to become more aware of a Spirit there. The flow of information is better and they are much more trusting and confident. This applies to you in your mediumship as well.

You must always be in a relaxed or meditative state where you are open and focused. A focused mind is a powerful thing in mediumship because it blocks out your own internal chatter and makes you aware of the Spirit communication. Your logic will interject and make you question if what you are receiving is real. Don't pay any mind to this. Remember any impression that is persistent and reoccurring is definitely an impression from the Spirit World.

You want to be a clear channel of communication for the Spirit world. If your mind is constantly wandering and feeding into your own rational thoughts, mental chatter or insecurities you won't be able to feel much from the Spirit.

Our rational mind and logic is used to being the spokesperson for our daily activities. For the purpose of mediumship and spiritual practices, the use of discipline and training will force our rational mind to take the backseat while our intuition drives.

Mind Focus Exercise: Choose a color to focus on. Now close your eyes and visualize that color. You can set a timer to practice this for 45-60 seconds. If thoughts enter your mind let them and release them. Practice focusing on a different color at least three times for 45-60 seconds each.

You can also concentrate on a weather/flower in your mind. For example, imagine a storm coming in. Feel and experience the storm. Practice this for at least 45-60 seconds. Now switch to a different weather such as a warm sunny day or a brisk cool autumn day. These exercises will help you to ignore mental chatter and concentrate specifically on the task which will aid you in mediumship connections.

Chapter 6: Creating Your Spiritual Toolbox Kit

As you develop in your spiritual journey, it is important to have a spiritual toolbox kit. This is something you will fall back and will help you immensely.

What is a spiritual toolbox kit? This is a kit of resources, spiritual tools and rituals that help you daily with personal awareness and soul development. It will aid you in having a deeper connection to your intuition and also to the Spirit World. As you grow and expand so does your awareness and relationship of the Spirit World.

In a spiritual toolbox kit you will discover what helps you relax, centered, grounded, open, receptive and aware of higher knowledge and inner wisdom. Everyone has different tools and there is no right, wrong or perfect kit. Think of this as your own personal spiritual prescription. Here is an example of what is in my Spiritual Toolbox Kit.

1. **Meditation-** Meditation helps me to clear my mind and tap into my inner wisdom. By meditating I am able to release anxiety or stress and communicate with my Spirit Guides for guidance if needed. Meditation opens my awareness to the Spirit World and allows me to deepen my connection to a divine source.

    Meditation works for some people and for others it doesn't. See how it works for you and decide for yourself. There are so many types of meditations available on YouTube. You can look for a meditation on anything such as anxiety, meeting your Spirit Guide, abundance or healing. Practice the type of meditation you feel drawn to and put it in your kit.

2. **Exercise**- Running and physical exercise is my own personal therapy. I also feel like I release a lot of stress and concerns during exercise. With exercising I can tune out and tune into my body, mind and soul. It's my quiet time and escape from the world. This can also be a spiritual practice such as through yoga, walking or tai chi.

If you aren't keen on exercising in the gym perhaps walking outside or cleaning the house will help you relax and clear your mind. Find a healthy active outlet or join a group/class that resonates with you. This will definitely help you overall and spiritually.

3. **Healthy Eating & Proper Nutrition**- It is said "You are what you eat" and personally I can tell a big difference in my energy with the food I eat. When we digest heavier food we tend to feel slower and heavier. When we eat lighter it reflects in our energy level and mood.

When it comes to doing any type of spiritual work, it is suggested that before you meditate, work with a client or practice mediumship exercises you should eat light so that you aren't feeling low in energy. Think about it. Would you eat something very heavy right before doing any physical exercise such as running? You would probably eat a light snack or have a bigger lunch to burn off the carbs later after digesting. The same applies to mediumship. Being mindful of diet and nutrition will help you in all aspects of life including your own spiritual practice.

4. **Tools of Relaxation**- Soft meditative music, candles, and incense or aromatherapy oils can definitely help me relax after a stressful day. I also enjoy taking a nice hot shower and imagining all of the energy from my day being washed away down the drain. What helps you relax after a stressful day or week? Some people like a hot cup of tea or reading a good book. Massage therapy, acupuncture or going to the spa are also great outlets.

When you take time out for yourself with some personal self-care rituals whether it's placing lavender under your pillow to help you fall asleep or listening to some meditation in the music to center you before starting the day it will have a positive effect. You are taking the time to ground yourself and clear your mind of any toxic or residual energy.

When you release this you become more open, aware and receptive to communicating with the Spirit World and to your higher self. Always make time to take care of yourself even if for just 5 minutes a day.

5. **Nature**- When I spend time outside even just to take my dog for a nice evening walk I can feel a difference in my mood and well-being. I feel more grounded and my thoughts are clear. Nature also helps us to become more aware of our surroundings and the energy of plant life.

We become more attune to the energy of the Earth and the natural wonders of existence. Spending time in nature will deepen your connection to a world outside of you and also open your chakras. You may feel more inspired or a sense of Spirit. Shamans are known to connect with the elemental and nature spirits accessing higher wisdom and knowledge. Practice spending time outside with yourself not texting or listening to music. Just walk, observe and take in the experience.

6. **Creativity & Spiritual Journaling**- In my Spiritual Toolbox Kit I carry the gift of writing and journaling. I have always been really creative since I was a child and I find writing soothes my emotions and allows me to express myself in a unique and positive way.

Creativity activates your imagination and journaling allows you to write without boundaries, limits or expectations. If you aren't a really creative person think of other activities that you enjoy. Some people have told me they love to organize their home or cook new recipes. Anything that is already a natural hobby or interests you, practice doing more of it.

Exercise #1: Obtain a journal. You can go to any bookstore or a regular notebook is fine. I would suggest finding a journal that resonates with you. Some people like leather-bound journals and others like graphics with neat designs. This journal will be yours to document any inspirational thoughts, psychic feelings, dreams and Spiritual experiences with mediumship or anything else. This journal will help you along your life journey.

Exercise #2: Take a moment to write down your personal Spiritual Toolbox Kit. Think about what works for you. Remember the list above is mine and yours doesn't have to look like it at all. What practices and rituals already work for you to feel more grounded, less stressed or spiritually aware? This kit will be your own personal box of spiritual practices that you can use anytime and add to or modify.

Chapter 7: Sensing Spirit

Communicating with spirit requires us to use our psychic senses but the information doesn't come from a physical environment, person or object. The information comes from Spirit and is communicated through several or one of our paraphysical senses.

Paraphysical defined by Merriam-Webster Dictionary as resembling physical phenomena but without physical cause. Therefore when we receive information through a paraphysical sense it may feel real but isn't physically present.

An example of this feeling as if you connect with a Spirit who passed away and suddenly have the sense of pain in your chest. This could mean you are actually experiencing pain in the chest or the Spirit is giving you the feeling of chest to convey information about his/her passing such as a heart attack.

The following paraphysical senses are:

1. **Clairvoyance**- This sense is the ability to see images, colors, visuals or scenes similarly described as watching a movie trailer in your mind's eye (center of forehead area). Mediums will often see the impression of a Spirit's face, body or life with their clairvoyance and describe it in visual detail.

This type of clairvoyance is subjective and only experienced by the medium communicating with Spirit.

Objective clairvoyance is physically seeing the spirit or physical phenomena with your eyesight and may also be experienced by other people in the room as well.

2. **Clairsentience**- The ability to sense Spirit energetically through touch, feeling or temperature change. This is often described as a "knowing" in which the medium simply knows there is a Spirit around them trying to communicate.

   You may feel changes in body temperature, or physical sensations such as a rapid heartbeat, butterflies in your stomach or a breeze/touch around your face or hair.

3. **Clairaudience**- The ability to hear Spirit communicating to you through thought or sensation around your ears. This is a rare type of sense but also a very unique one.

   Sometimes in the beginning stages of clairaudient development people experience a buzzing or ringing around their ears. The medium may also "hear" a stream of thoughts entering their inner ear area into their mind.

There is also objective clairaudience in which a Spirit's voice manifests in a physical environment and is heard by all such as in a séance. They may communicate a message to the audience or simply greet everyone.

Clairaudience is not to be confused with hallucinations or delusional thinking in which a person believes someone is there talking to them. You are able to differentiate between reality with clairaudience whereas someone who suffers from this type of mental illness struggles to see the difference between reality and non-reality.

4. **Clairscent**- The ability to smell scents or aromas from Spirit. These scents or smells are not physically present where other people can smell it and is only experienced by the medium.

   An example of this is when a medium may suddenly get a strong smell of cigarettes when communicating with a person who passed from lung cancer.

5. **Clairgustance**- The ability to taste substances such as food or drink from Spirit. These impressions are quick and linger to communicate something about the Spirit communicating.

An example of this is if a medium is communicating with a man who owned a pizza restaurant. She/he may get the taste of warm melted mozzarella with tomato sauce. The Spirit is giving the medium that impression to convey a piece of information about his passion for Italian food, pizza or cultural background.

All these senses are subjectively experienced and are not physically present to the medium or other people.

6. **Spirit Energy**- When I refer to Spirit in the book I am talking about a higher vibrational Spirit Guide or a passed loved one. I only set the intention to work with higher loving spirits. If you are feeling a negative presence than I would suggest you first practice grounding and protecting yourself before beginning any type of mediumship communication. It would be best to avoid trying spirit communication until you are stronger spiritually and intuitively.

Chapter 8: Recognizing How Spirits Communicate

A Spirit Impression is a feeling, sense, image or random awareness that a spirit is communicating to you. The following are common ways to recognize a spirit impression.

Spirit Impressions

- Persistent feeling or thought of a presence
- Interrupts your train of thought; There is no external stimulation or trigger from your environment and may enter your consciousness out of the blue.
- May manifest randomly or spontaneously at first; you may sense Spirit randomly without trying.
- Sudden image or memory of passed loved one may come to mind out of nowhere
- Temperature change; you may feel ice cold or very hot and it may come on one side of your body or all over.
- Body sensations not attributed to a physical health issue, i.e. racing heart, shallow breath, tightness in chest
- Tingling sensation in your body or in your hands or arms

- Heaviness in the air or a lightness in being; you may suddenly feel a heavy energy around you or feel lighter than usual.

When you open up to Spirit you will notice these subtle impressions and become more aware of them with practice. Meditation will help you to become more sensitive and conscious of Spirit impressions.

Chapter 9: Common Signs from Spirit

1. **Dreams**– The most common form of communication and sign from Spirit are dreams. In our dream state we are more open and receptive. Our spirit may leave our body during the sleep state and travel to other spiritual dimensions. In these dimensions we will connect with passed loved ones and Spirit guides.

    How can you tell if your dream was an actual connection with the Spirit World? One way to differentiate between your own subconscious and Spirit is if the dream felt real or not. When the dream is extremely vivid and real as if actually happened then it was a definite sign of Spirit communication also known as a "visitation".

2. **Music & Sounds**- Often Spirit Guides and passed loved ones will try to catch our attention with a particular song or sound to let us know they are around and giving a message to us.

    I remember I was grocery shopping and a random song came on that reminded me of my uncle who passed many years ago. Later that same week I heard the same song again while ordering coffee. I felt this persistent sense that he was around trying to send my Mother a message so I called her. She told me the anniversary of his death was in a few days confirming my sense of his presence around.

The next time you hear a random song or sound that reminds you of your passed loved one or of a Spirit Guide, don't dismiss it! Listen and pay attention to what he/she may be trying to tell you. Sometimes the message is as simple as just letting you know he/she is there.

3. **Scents**– Clients have told me that after their loved one has died they sometimes smell their favorite perfume or cologne around. Spirits will communicate their favorite scents such as a perfume or favorite food, flower or vice, i.e. cigarettes. One client lost his wife in a tragic house fire and after occasionally would smell burning smoke whenever she was around him.

4. **Animals**– Our Spirit loved ones do like to get our attention through our pets so the next time you see your cat or dog staring at something in the corner or barking for no reason you may want to consider it possible Spirit Communication.

5. **Moved/missing Objects**– I always found this form of communication to be comical. A few clients have told me that special objects significant to their loved one went missing such as the family recipes or a piece of jewelry. Sometimes your passed loved one will actually move an item from one place to another as a sure way to get your attention.

   The movie *Ghost* with Demi Moore and Whoopi Goldberg is actually a very accurate description of how our loved ones transition sometimes and find clever ways in which they will try to get our attention such as moving objects or flickering lights.

6. **Electricity**- Spirit will catch your attention through electricity such as flickering lights, radio static or the television turning off and on. I have also heard of phenomena with cell phones where the phone turns off/on at a specific time during the day.

7. **Symbols & Reoccurring Numbers**- A strong common form of Spirit Communication are symbols and number sequences. An example of this is when my student connects with her native American Spirit Guide she will always see a feather headdress first. This symbol is his signal to her that he is ready to communicate.

As Spirit loved ones blend their energy with yours you may receive symbols in your mind's eye or third eye chakra area. You may suddenly see colors/images, hear words/thoughts, sense a taste in your mouth or smell scents. This isn't your mind playing tricks on you.

This is the Spirit giving you information about them for you to understand. They will use all 5 of your paraphysical senses to convey details about themselves and their life to help you verify this to your client. Someone I know lost her mother on November 11, 2011 so whenever she sees 1111 or 11:11 she knows it's her mother saying hi to her.

When preparing to work with Spirit it is important to be aware of some sure signs and signal of Spirit communication.

Be mindful of any random, spontaneous, subtle symbols, feelings or anything out of the ordinary when working with spirit. If it is a persistent feeling, thought or impression you want to definitely take note of it or share it with your partner or client.

8. **Temperature changes**- This is one noticeable sign a Spirit loved one is beginning to blend with your auric energy. You will feel a change in your own body temperature and may feel warmer or colder than usual.

9. **Body Tingling & Sensations**- When sending the thought out to Spirit that you are ready to work you may feel spontaneous sensations like a tingling in your hands or light touch around your head. Some students say one side of their body went a little numb or their heart started to beat a little faster than usual.

   You may feel a tightness in your chest or butterflies in your stomach. These sensations are not permanent but just a way for Spirit to get your attention to let you know they are beginning to work with you.

10. **Memories**- One important signal from Spirit is the use of memories to communicate information about them. For example, let's say as you are connecting with Spirit you suddenly see a memory of your childhood best friend pop into your mind and remember how he/she died suddenly in an accident.

    This doesn't mean your best friend is actually there communicating with you but that the

Spirit is using this memory about your life because he/she was a childhood best friend of the person you are reading for and died in a similar way. Any memories or information related to your life could very well relate to the Spirit you are communicating with. They use our memories and knowledge to give information about themselves.

I like to think of communicating with Spirit loved ones as putting a puzzle together. You receive pieces of information and slowly put it all together to see the Spirit person's life story.

Signals & Signs Exercise: In your journal or on a piece of paper I want you to bring into your mind someone close to you that died. If you don't have anyone close to you who passed then think of a close best friend or relative who I alive. Concentrate on that person's energy for a minute.

Write down his/her physical features, relationship to you and how they passed (if they did). Reflect on any memories that stand out between you and this person. Think about the person's personality and behaviors, favorite activities and hobbies.

If the person is passed send a thought out to him/her to come join you in this exercise just for a brief moment. If the person isn't passed then take your awareness to him/her and see if you can feel what he/she may be doing. Reflect and listen for a couple of minutes. Do you feel any body sensations? Are there any other symbols/signals you are receiving without thinking about them? Do you feel his/her spirit? Write down your impressions.

Chapter 10: Setting Your Intention & Protection

The first thing to know when practicing evidential mediumship or any type of Spiritual work is setting your intention and protection. What does that exactly mean?

Setting your intention is knowing what you are intending to do, why you are doing it and stating it in your mind as well as in your actions.

For example, when I prepare for a session with a client in my mind I always set the intention that I am working for the highest good of all including the Spirit World and that I only intend to communicate with Spirits of a positive and high vibration. I also intend to communicate messages of healing and guidance to my client. I say a protection prayer and do a visualization to ensure my space and energy are protected and safe.

When setting your intention it's always important to remember to come from a clear and positive state. It is never a good idea to start any type of spiritual work in a distressed, negative or low energy state.

Don't force yourself if you are having an off day to practice mediumship or any other spiritual practice. It is similar to exercise, "Don't compromise your form." Sometimes we need to take that as a caution sign to step back and reassess ourselves so that we can go back to it in a better state that will benefit everyone including ourselves.

I remember something a teacher told me in my mediumship development class "Whenever you have a day of doing any type of spiritual work be it meditation or seeing clients you must always leave any personal baggage at the door." When we are feeling negative or low this blocks us from receiving clear information and working with the Spirit World.

Our own stuff may affect our connection and we may not be able to deliver information clearly or strongly. Your personal issues could end up being projected onto that person and negatively affecting the reading.

For your own sake remember to take steps to set your intention, clearing residual energy and protecting yourself before any Spirit communication, spiritual exercise or practice and just in your daily life.

Setting Your Intention Exercise: When doing Spirit Communication, mediumship or meditation think about your intention. Why are you doing this and what do you hope for? What are your intentions? For example before my session I would say "I intend to work with passed loved ones for the person I am reading for." Remember you always want to set a positive intention and of the highest vibration. Write down a few statements of positive intentions and always state those in your mind before doing mediumship or spiritual practice.

Protection Exercise: Before you do any work it is extremely important you protect yourself energetically. Since we are all energy and mediums especially are sensitive to all types of energy a protection prayer and meditation will help you feel more centered and close off from unwanted energies.

Practice this protection visualization: Take a few long deep breaths and exhale out any tension. Move your awareness to the bottoms of your feet and imagine roots coming out from beneath them grounding you like a tree to Mother Earth. Now scan your body from head to toe and look for any toxic or blocked energy.

Each time you feel a blockage take a deep breath in and release it. As you exhale this energy out say in your head "I release any unwanted or toxic energy and invite love and positive light in." Now visualize a bright golden light at the top of your head like the rays of the sun beaming down on you. This light protects you and keeps you safe.

You can say a prayer of protection now asking for your Spirit loved ones and Guides to keep you safe while you meditate, practice mediumship or whenever you just need to feel protected.

White Light of Protection Exercise

This is another useful exercise to protect you and also become aware of Spirit energy.

1. Close your eyes and get into a comfortable sitting position.
2. Take a few deep breaths in and hold them for about 5 seconds. With each exhale imagine the tension in your face or body leaving and sinking down into the earth.
3. Begin to focus on your breath and imagine a ball of white light at the center of your core. This white light helps protects and connect you to divine source energy.
4. Imagine this light expanding and filling you from head to toe.
5. Know that you are safe and always connected to Spirit with this light. Allow yourself to sit in this energy.
6. When you're ready you can open your eyes and come back to the room. Write down what you experienced and be aware of any impressions or signals received for future exercises.

Chapter 11: What's Your Type?

As you work with your mediumistic ability, you will also recognize what type of control you have with the Spirit World. There are three levels of control with Spirit Communication.

1. **Low Control**- This person is very empathic and may respond quickly and emotionally to Spirit. They have a hard time separating their own emotions, issues or ego from mediumship. An example of this type of person is someone who is very sensitive and responds to all types of Spirits anywhere at any time from home to work.

   Remember, you are in the physical body and Spirit isn't. This is a relationship just in the same way you are in relationships with your friends and family. If you are too sensitive to Spirit then you have to place some boundaries.

   Spirit will respect you and understand they have to communicate with you when it's more appropriate for your lifestyle.

2. **Medium Control**- This person is somewhat developed in their mediumistic ability and may be able to connect sometimes to Spirit but not always when they want to. They may receive mediumship impressions randomly or

spontaneously such as going to dinner with a friend and feeling their friend's deceased Mother around them trying to communicate a message.

This type of link just happens whenever without the person trying to connect with Spirit.

3. **High Control**- This person is a much more experienced medium and can turn their ability off/on whenever they choose. They are able to tune in and out to Spirit energy at will.

You may start out at a low/medium control and through practice and training your level of control will change. As you evolve so does your relationship with the Spirit World. Remember your boundaries and trust Spirit will respect that and communicate with you at the appropriate times.

Chapter 12: Sitting with Spirit & Making Contact

One of the most important aspects about mediumship is having the patience and concentration to simply sit with Spirit.

Sitting with Spirit is the essence to making a strong link and successful contact for any reading you give. When you sit with Spirit you allow yourself the experience to just be aware of the Spirit World without any other purpose but to feel this divine energy.

Remember if you have positive intentions to connect with the Spirit World you will get positive results meaning your experience will be eye-opening and expanding. There is nothing to be afraid of when working with the Spirit World. I have heard many stories about people who could see Spirits but became very afraid and then "Turned it off".

Our passed loved ones and Spirit Guides don't want to frighten us or make us uncomfortable. They only want to communicate and give us the pleasure of being able to feel their presence again in a different form. It's a beautiful gift and one that we should never be afraid of.

If you do get uncomfortable at the thought of sitting with Spirit remember to do your grounding and protecting exercises. I encourage you to set boundaries with the Spirit World and develop a relationship with them just like any other relationship in your life.

Take time to sit and talk to your Spirit Team and let them know when you are interested in communication. You can set the boundary to have communication during practice exercises or in meditation but not before you go to sleep. I know many people who had trouble sleeping because they would feel the presence of Spirit around.

You are the one in control and always in the higher. They will understand and come to you when the time is more appropriate.

Sitting with Spirit is similar to meditation and is often described as sitting in the power which means you are in a slight relaxed or altered state but you have a focused and aware mind. With meditation it is a little different because the purpose is to still the mind so it is a very passive state.

Being with Spirit requires you to be more aware and active as the Spirit World draws close to you to communicate. Think of it as sitting and hanging out with a close friend or relative for a little while without exchanging a lot of conversation. You are aware of each other and may sense things intuitively about one another without even speaking.

Sitting with Spirit Exercise: Get into a relaxed and grounded state. Make sure to set your intention and protect yourself. Now visualize in your mind an elevator. See yourself enter the elevator and press the button to the top floor. As you rise further up feel the change in your energy. Send a thought out to the Spirit World that you'd like to spend time with them for a while. Ask them to draw close to you and to blend their energy with yours. Don't look to engage in conversation but mainly for them to make you aware of their presence.

Now as the doors of the elevator open find a comfortable spot in the room and sit down. Across from you is another empty chair. Close your eyes and wait. Wait for Spirit to come into your energy and invite them to sit down in the chair across from you. Stay in this state of awareness for at least 5-10 minutes. Notice any subtle changes in your body and emotionally. When you are done come back into the room and thank Spirit for spending time with you. Write down your experiences.

You can practice this every day for a 5-10 minutes or a few times a week. The point is to build your relationship with the Spirit World and be in silence with them for a little while similar to when monks meditate together.

Spirit Awareness Exercise

As you begin to work with Spirit, it is important that to develop an awareness of Spirit energy. I would recommend you record this exercise on your phone or any audio-recording device to play it back later.

1. Close your eyes and get into a comfortable sitting position.
2. Just as we did in the protection exercise before, take a moment to enter a meditative state.

3. When you are more relaxed, imagine you are in a tube of shimmering white light connecting you to the Spirit World.
4. Set the intention in your mind that you would like to sense Spirit.
5. Once you've set your intention shift your awareness to your solar plexus or center of *clairsentience*. Notice any body sensations.
6. Now move your awareness to your heart center. You may feel as if your heart is beating a little faster than usual or some emotions may come that weren't present before.
7. Continue to move up to the throat center. How does the energy feel here?
8. And up to the center of your forehead or *clairvoyance* center. Talk to Spirit and ask them to show you an image or word. You may see a face, symbol or color.
9. Now move your awareness to your ears or *clairaudience* center. Do you hear any sounds or words?
10. Lastly, move your awareness to the top of your head or crown chakra area. Do you notice a denser energy around you or by the top of your head?
11. Sit with the awareness of Spirit for a couple of minutes. Feel and notice any sensations or impressions.
12. When you are ready bring yourself back to the room and open your eyes.

Write down what you experienced and thank Spirit for coming. These exercises will help you to sense when a Spirit is trying to communicate with you.

Chapter 13: Talking to Spirit

Now that we've discussed how to use your psychic senses with mediumship and how to recognize spirit impressions and signs, you are ready for the next step; communication with Spirit.

With every new skill in life there is a method to be learned. This also applies to mediumship.

Whether you are a novice student or advanced, it is important you have a foundation to begin to work with Spirit. Our psychic and mediumistic abilities are like muscles, the more we practice using them the stronger and better we become at it.

One key factor to remember is mediumship is literally the mirror of our mind meaning Spirit will work with your knowledge & awareness of life, personal experiences, and memories to communicate information about themselves.

So basically the more you know, the better instrument you will be for the Spirit world!

For example, if you went to medical school and researched extensive information on cures for cancer you may attract Spirits who passed of cancer or some related cause.

It's like a signal goes off in the Spirit World that this medium went to school for medicine and studied cancer so it may be easier to work with you than a medium who studied law or architecture.

You become a beacon of knowledge and a channel to be used by Spirit to communicate information to their loved ones still alive or to a group of people to raise the consciousness of humanity.

Spirit knows what your soul make-up is and can access any information about you in your aura or energy field. Our auras contains our life history, personal experiences, soul DNA and more.

All Spirit has to do is blend with your energy field to know if you are the perfect channel to communicate through. This is similar to the law of attraction or like-attracts-like. The same way we tend to attract similar people in our waking life applies to attracting like-minded Spirits.

In my personal experience as a medium, I have a close relative who suffers with a severe mental illness and for a few months I attracted Spirit people who had passed through suicide or suffered from mental illness.

I believe Spirit knew I was a strong enough channel to communicate with these types of souls and therefore chose me as a conduit to speak with the family and friends left behind.

Something else I've learned in my experience is You Don't Choose Spirit, Spirit Chooses You! Remember whether you are communicating with a passed loved one or a Spirit Guide, these people existed at one point in time and are depending on you to be the channel.

The following exercise is a great method that I learned in one of my training classes and found it to be extremely helpful.

Some of my students have found this method helpful and others have their own formats of spirit communication that works perfectly for them. Whatever way works for you, use it! Remember the idea is to simply get into a grounded neutral state and become aware of Spirit.

This method is a simple exercise that sends a signal to Spirit that you are ready and willing to work with them. You may use this exercise when you want to practice evidential mediumship with passed loved ones, channeling, or communicate with a Spirit Guide.

Opening to Spirit Exercise

1. **Relax and Center**- Relax your mind and body in whatever way works best for you. You may want to take a couple of long deep breaths and release tension in your facial muscles, neck and shoulders area.
2. **Expand your Energy**- Now expand your energy by visualizing a golden ball of light at the center of your core. Visualize this ball of

light expanding out to the Spirit World and see it touching the depths of the universe.
3. **Set your Intention**- Set your intention that you are ready and willing to communicate with Spirit.
4. **Allow Spirit In**- Now allow Spirit energy to draw near to you. You may feel subtle sensations or impressions. This process is a blending of their Spirit energy with yours.
5. **Ask**- Ask Spirit to come close to you as if they are stepping into your own shoes. You can also visualize a door behind you and them stepping through that door.
6. **Instrument of Energy**- Allow your body to be used as a tool. Pay attention to any feelings or sudden body sensations. As they blend with you, remember your body may feel different.
7. **Be Open**- Stay open to what you are receiving. Remember this information is not coming from you, but through you. You are the channel.
8. **Message**- What is the Spirit saying? Notice for details or information.
9. **Conclusion**- Come back to the room you are sitting in and thank the Spirit for coming.

Chapter 14: Telling the Story of Your Spirit Loved One

When you are practicing evidential mediumship and connecting with passed loved ones, a key factor in having a successful connection are details. A sitter wants to know if his/her loved one is really communicating with them and the only way to really verify that is by providing evidence or details that the sitter would understand.

Consider this like painting the picture of the Spirit Loved One communicating with you. You are slowly telling the story about this person and their life. I often describe it to my clients as putting a puzzle together. I get tiny impressions or puzzle pieces and bit by bit I put it all together to create the story of this person.

Remember you are communicating with real people. They had lives, families, careers and so much more. As a medium you are a channel of communication for them to funnel this information to you.

As you practice your mediumship abilities will become stronger, in depth and detailed.

To start here are some solid pieces of evidence you should always bring in first before trying to uncover more details.

1. **Sex of the Spirit**- Are they male/female? It is always important to immediately identify if the spirit is a male/female.
2. **Type of Passing**- How did they die? Feel out the energy of their passing. Always ask if you

have trouble. Did they pass in their elderly years? Tragically either by an accident, suicide or murder? Illness-related such as cancer or a life-threatening disease? Pay attention to any subtle body changes when you are looking for cause of death as this is indication that he/she may have had health issues in this area.

3. **Age**- Does the Spirit feel old or young to you? The spirit will give you an impression of their age to indicate how old they were when they passed or sometimes their more favorited years. They may show you a memory of them when they are in their 40s married and in love because that was a special time of their life or because the client may recognize the memory. They may also be older when they passed but have a young spirit. Age can be tricky so be mindful of how to interpret it. Always remember if you get stuck or confused, ask for more clarity.

4. **Relationship to the Client**- You want to know who the person is to your client so you would look for what their relationship may be. Does it feel like a relative such as a parent/grandparent/sibling? Or do you sense a more intimate relationship like a best friend/spouse/partner?

Sometimes it doesn't feel like a very close relationship at all. It may be a distant relative or a colleague just passing through to say hello or give a message. Don't dismiss it and just try your best to work with the information you are receiving,

Now that we have covered basic details which should always be your list of details to check off when connecting with Spirit let's move on to more advanced evidence.

1. **Personality**- When you are connecting with Spirit you want to get a feel for his/her personality. Have you ever been to a medium and he/she starts to act like your passed loved one in the session? A medium is very sensitive to the characteristics of the Spirit communicating with them and may start to behave or talk similar (not intentionally) but as a form of channeling to convey the Spirit's personality or characteristics. I have been told sometimes that I sound just like the client's passed relative or am sitting just like him/her.

   Be mindful of personality changes and if you feel differently. Notice subtle body shifts and how you're sitting, positioning your hands or behaving. You may feel quirkier, quieter or bolder. These are all details and signals about the Spirit's personality, behavior or quirks when he/she was alive.

2. **Physical Features**- What did the person look like? Notice if you feel larger in physical size or smaller in frame. If I am communicating

with a more petite person I tend to feel much smaller in size and the same if I am talking to someone who was tall or heavier built.

You may notice the color of the person's hair, facial features, eye color, scars and other details like tattoos. Look for the basics first. Tall/short, heavier/slim, hair & eye color, glasses/contacts. You can go into further detail once you cover your basics.

3. **Career/Life Purpose**- Find out what the person did for work when he/she was alive. Look for symbols related to work. A desk may mean he/she had a 9-5 job or an apron/kitchenware could represent a housewife or homemaker. Did the person work many jobs or have one single job their entire life? Was it more business or a service-related field? Ask questions and get to know the person you are communicating with.

4. **Hobbies**- What were the person's hobbies outside of family or work? Did they enjoy gardening or playing a sport? Some Spirits show me they loved to BBQ, play golf or go to the beach. Other Spirits may enjoy writing, creative arts or collecting things. These are great pieces of evidence and can really help with identifying who the person may be to your sitter.

5. **Pets**- I love asking the person I'm communicating with about pets. Sometimes the person shows me their favorite pet who is now with them in the Spirit World. Other times they didn't like animals and preferred to not have a pet. Be sure to ask and look for any pets he/she may have had. You may actually feel the pet there with you if the animal also passed away.

6. **Military Service**- One key detail is discovering your Spirit person was in the military. Find out if you can what branch of service and around what age were they in. They sometimes even show you what kind of job they had as well.

7. **Scars, Surgeries & Injuries**- In my mediumship-now I like to look and ask for any particular surgeries or scars he/she may have had. The person may show me a surgery around a certain area of the body or a scar somewhere indicating an injury. If you can't get it clearly don't worry. In time you be able to receive more information and identify these details more clearly. Communicating with the Spirit World isn't an exact science and it takes time, dedication and practice.

8. **Special Memories**- Often times a Spirit person will show you unique memories shared with their loved one. You are also welcome to ask about any striking or memorable times shared

between your sitter and their Spirit loved one. They may show you special holidays, birthdays or anniversaries, trips and vacations.

These memories actually help to build a strong connection to the Spirit person and brings a sense of life to the reading. Your sitter may actually feel as if he/she is literally there sharing that memory with them again. What a beautiful gift to give and be a part of.

9. **Life on the Other Side-** Your Spirit person may show you what they have been up to since they passed away and what life is like on the other side. You are encouraged to ask and see what they show you. He/she may be helping people, working on projects or spending time with other passed loved ones in Spirit. Find out if he/she is with any other deceased relatives that your sitter could possibly know about or identify.

It's so great to give messages from more than one Spirit person and really brings a lot of comfort to the person hearing it. Don't be afraid to find out and ask.

10. **Updates on the Sitter's Life-** When a Spirit person passes away one thing they love to talk about is what the sitter has been up to since he/she died. They may talk about new relationships in the sitter's life, job changes,

relocation, family concerns and other new developments.

This is especially comforting because it shows that we truly never die and can still be around influencing our family and loved ones even in Spirit form.

As you develop further in your mediumship your evidence will get stronger and more detailed. One of the ways in which you can make your mediumship stronger is by meditating at least once a day in whatever format resonates with you. Some people enjoy listening to guided meditations where they can meet with a Spirit Guide.

Other meditations are focused more on stilling the mind and reaching a state of deep relaxation. Deepak Chopra & Oprah have tons of great meditation series on all types of topics such as love, abundance, finances and others. I suggest exploring meditation and seeing what practice resonates with you.

Other types of meditation include physical exercise, yoga, swimming or spending time in nature. Be sure to always take at least 10 minutes before or after any type of meditation to set your intention and sit with the Spirit World. This is extremely beneficial in your mediumship and gives you the opportunity to perhaps discover some deeper wisdom that you can't always access in your waking life.

Exercise: This exercise is best practiced with a partner so if you are able to find a friend or relative who would be willing to work with you then this is great. Otherwise I would suggest joining a spiritual Facebook group and seeing if you could practice with someone there.

Have your partner tell you the name of a passed loved one including when he/she passed away. Take a moment to ground yourself and move your awareness to the Spirit World. Once you begin to feel a shift energetically send a thought out to this Spirit person and ask him/her to join you in communication.

As you feel this Spirit person blend with you take a moment to notice any signals or signs you may be receiving. Now begin to communicate with him/her and remember to start off with basic details as I mentioned earlier. You want to look for the sex of the Spirit (male/female), Type of passing, Age and the relationship to your partner. Once you find out these details feel free to share with your partner what you are receiving and look for further details if you want.

Lastly don't forget to find out what your Spirit person wants to say. What is the message?

You are encouraged to practice this exercise with other partners. Be sure to state your basic details first before moving into anything further. If you aren't able to verify who it is right away keep practicing and remember mediumship isn't a science. When you let go and trust you will have successful links. Many times we are the ones blocking the information from flowing smoothly and clearly.

Chapter 15: How to Interpret Symbols from Spirit

As you develop spiritually a common theme that occurs in development are symbols. When you are using your intuition or practicing mediumship you will almost always receive symbols.

Symbols are also commonly used in our everyday life such as the American Flag representing the United States or patriotism, a black cat could mean bad or good luck depending on someone's belief system, and a red rose could symbolize romance or love. There are tons of symbols used to communicate a message in our cultures, subcultures, families, careers and so on.

It is exactly the same when practicing mediumship or any type of spiritual healing. Artists use symbols all the time in their work to convey a meaning or give a message about something. In the case with mediumship, Spirit people will use symbols to communicate messages about themselves, family or other matters.

Just in the same way symbols are subject to interpretation based on a person's belief system it applies also to any symbol received in mediumship. For example, you grew up raised in a specific religious faith so a Spirit person may show you a cross to indicate that he/she was also raised of the same faith or held the same beliefs about a particular religion.

Symbols mean different things for each person just in the same way colors, patterns or numbers do. They are all subject to interpretation and there is no right or wrong way of interpreting a symbol you receive from Spirit. It is all based on the feeling you get behind the symbol or a message.

For example, whenever I see the color pink in someone's energy I immediately feel it could mean several things either innocence, new beginnings such as a new love interest or healing on a deep level for new love to come in.

However, if you were to see the color pink you may have a different interpretation. The same applies to any other symbol. Some common symbols I have noticed people receive in mediumship are specific type of clothes, weather, colors and jewelry.

A Spirit may show you he/she dressed up in business wear which could indicate the type of work he/she was in when alive. Clothing can also reflect specific personality traits such as very reserved, proper, well-mannered or possibly good with finances.

If you saw weather such as sunny/rainy day this could mean the Spirit had either a very bright or moody personality. If you saw a color the Spirit person may be trying to communicate the nature of a relationship with someone be it romantic, family or co-worker.

Colors could also mean mood, characteristics, or financial status. Some people think of green as the color for money where other people see it as the color of healing or growth.

When you practice mediumship there is no right or wrong interpretation to the symbol you are receiving from the Spirit. Sometimes you may get confused about what it actually means and should ask for more information about the symbol to better interpret it.

Everything we receive about symbols is very rarely literal. About 10% of it is actually literal where 90% is symbolic.

Whenever you receive a symbol try to ask your higher self or inner voice what the symbol could mean. Remember symbols can have more than one meaning and it is up to you to interpret it to the best of your ability.

A spirit may give you tightness in your chest as a symbol that he/she died of a heart attack, show you cigarettes because he/she liked to smoke, tastes of food to indicate favorite foods or that he/she was a big foodie.

You will receive the symbols via your paraphysical senses which are clairvoyance, clairaudience, clairgustance, clairscent and clairsentience. I define these paraphysical senses further in my other book Psychic Development for Beginners: A Practical Guide to Developing your Intuition & Psychic Gifts.

With practice you will become better at interpreting symbols as well as faster to receive and understand what they mean.

For now here is a simple method to get you started on interpreting symbols when Spirit shows them to you.

Method for Symbol Interpretation

1. **Literal or Symbolic**- Ask the Spirit person is this symbol literal or symbolic? You may immediately feel that the symbol isn't literal and know what it means but in the case that you shouldn't don't be afraid to ask what it could mean.
2. **Strong Feelings**- Pay attention to the feelings or sensations that come when you are receiving the symbol. You may feel an emotion, physical change in your body or intuitive impression when you are interpreting this symbol. This will help to interpret it better and understand the message or meaning behind it.
3. **Expand**- Ask for more information if you get stuck on the symbol and are confused about the meaning. Every symbol has a meaning and tells a story. Often Spirit will give a message through a symbol and it is up to you to expand on this.
4. **Interpret**- Put the symbols together piece by piece. A student of mine had the symbol of a red telephone booth at a crossroads. Slowly she broke down each symbol and then put it all together.

The color red meant love/relationship, telephone booth was communication and crossroads was a turning point. Once she put it all together she realized the message was about a romantic relationship regarding communication and it reaching a turning point or crossroads.

5. **Message**- Lastly, find out what the message is behind the symbol. What is the Spirit person trying to tell you about it? Is it about his/her life when alive or about the sitter's? Don't be afraid to be wrong. You won't know unless you give the information and see if you were right or not. Better to know than to wonder plus not knowing hinders your spiritual growth intuitively and with the Spirit World.

    Messages contained in symbols could be a timeframe such as numbers or dates, an aspect of their life, family, personality, interests, job/career, values, location, hobbies and more.

Symbols Exercise:

In your journal, write down a few common symbols you are drawn to a lot. It could be a spiritual symbol such as a Buddha or Om sign, colors, patterns, numbers and anything else. Now write down any meanings or interpretations you associate with these symbols.

For example whenever I see the numbers 1212 I feel like Spirit is telling me I'm on the right path to a major transformation happening soon. Another symbol I am drawn to are rainbows which mean diversity and miracles. Mountains represents overcoming obstacles and rising above challenges.

Pay attention to some of your symbols and feel free to ask Spirit to use these symbols to indicate messages about themselves whenever they communicate with you.

Partner Symbol Exercise: Now with a partner I want you to practice working with symbols. Get into your grounded slightly meditative state and set the intention that you'd like to receive a symbol about this person. It could be a color, type of music or anything else that would be a representation of the person. Now shift your awareness to your third eye center and see what appears. You may see an actual scene or become aware of a symbol forming. Pay attention to any strong or persistent feelings that may arise. Share with your partner what you received and see if he/she understands it.

Spirit Symbols Exercise: This exercise is very similar to the one above except this time you are working with Spirit. Set the intention you'd like to communicate with a passed loved one related to your partner. Always be sure to get your basic details covered first; sex, age, type of passing and relationship to your partner. Now ask for a symbol that would represent the Spirit person in any way. Notice what you begin to receive and share.

Always write down any symbols you receive in your journal to remember for future reference should you encounter that symbol or another one similar. Consider it your very own spiritual symbols dictionary. You may even add more interpretations to one symbol over time and have a variety of meanings.

Chapter 16: Spirit Guides & How to Meet Yours

There are tons of concepts and ideas about spirit communication and mediumship. One common topic in mediumship is Spirit Guides. You may have heard of the term "spirit guide" or maybe you've never heard of this concept in your life.

Personally I had no clue what a Spirit Guide was until I took my first mediumship class. It was in my early development I discovered Spirit Guides existed.

So what is a Spirit Guide?

The first thing to know is all of us are born with a Spirit Guide. Spirits guides are believed to have existed at one point on the Earth but many years ago. They may existed during another time era or century as a common person or someone who served people such as a doctor, Native American Chief, tribe elder and so on.

Why do we have Spirit Guides?

Spirit Guides come to us throughout our lives to help us with a specific life lesson or help us accomplish a particular project or venture. They also assist us with special concerns or karmic patterns that need to be broken.

A Spirit Guide is meant to play the role of exactly a guide or teacher for you. You may have one main guide for a while and then receive another one at a different stage in your life. They are there to influence you on your journey to make better decisions and gravitate towards that which is meant for you. They may also help guide you towards those who can help you through difficult circumstances or life changes.

What kinds of guides do we have?

Guides can exists as wise teachers from long ago, higher vibrational beings such as Angels, and sometimes (very rarely) passed loved ones and friends.

Our passed loved ones do comfort and help us along our path but play different roles as they are also evolving on the other side in their journey.

What do guides help us with?

Guides have already evolved to such a state that they can assist and influence someone. They may have existed as one point as a shaman, healer or teacher and will influence someone who has these gifts in the same way.

A guide may have also experienced a lot of loss and trauma in their time on Earth and may go to someone who is experiencing heavy loss and trauma to help them recover.

Guides play different roles and will help us in various aspects of our lives such as career path, relationship direction, family karma, and soul lessons.

You can meet or feel your Spirit Guide in a meditative, hypnotic or dream state.

Meet Your Spirit Guide Exercise

1. Get into a comfortable position and allow your body to relax.
2. Take a few deep breaths in and exhale. With each exhale, imagine the tension in your body drifting away.
3. Move your awareness to the bottoms of your feet and visualize a golden energy coming in from Mother Earth filling you from your feet all the way to your head.
4. Take a moment to feel this energy throughout your body.
5. Now visualize in your mind this energy connecting you to the divine energy of the universe.
6. Imagine this light takes you on a mind journey to a place of peace and tranquility.
7. Visualize your favorite vacation spot or a beautiful destination.
8. Allow yourself to experience and sounds, sights, smells or sensations.
9. Perhaps you are near a beach, lake, mountain, a secret garden or forest.
10. Now imagine a sanctuary nearby in the distance. It may be a temple, house, or cottage. Go there.

11. This is your sanctuary. Enter inside and notice how the environment looks. There may be incense burning, crystals around or flowers to your liking.
12. As you explore your sanctuary you notice a presence in the room.
13. Go towards this presence. It may be a person, feeling, or other type of energy.
14. As you approach it, you feel an overwhelming sense of comfort and love.
15. Allow yourself to communicate with this energy. This is your guide.
16. It may emerge in a form unique to you. Let it be whatever it pleases. Experience the qualities, appearance and form of this guide.
17. It may be a male/female, color or have no sex or form at all.
18. Sit with this guide and communicate with it. Feel free to ask it questions such as its name or a message for you.
19. When you are ready you can thank your guide for coming to meet with you and know you can easily connect with him/her anytime you want.
20. When you are ready, open your eyes. Write down your impressions, what your sanctuary looked like and overall experience.

Feel free to practice this exercise once a week and see how the experience is similar and different each time.

Chapter 17: Automatic Writing & Trance Channeling

As you work with Spirit, another form of mediumship is automatic writing & trance channeling which is connecting with Spirit through thought and channeling messages or guidance with writing or with your voice.

Some well-known channels are the *Seth Speaks* books or *Esther Hicks with Abraham.* These channels are mediums who are able to move into an altered state known as trance and allow a Spirit Guide or team of Guides to communicate through them by using their voice or hand as the instrument of channel.

It isn't a form of possession or anything of the sort. The medium is in full control and needs to be fully-developed in his or her training ability to channel the spirit world in such a way.

Forms of channeling may be message work with an audience, writing a book or spiritual healing. For example a guide may use a medium to channel healing to people with health issues. A spirit team of guides may also work with the medium to send a message to humanity to wake consciousness or bring forward a new philosophy of thinking.

When I first witnessed trance channeling I was in shock and utterly impressed. The medium has to surrender completely to the process and trust that the information will come through without fear or judgment.

There is always a positive intention stated before the medium enters trance and it is considered to be a very old-school or traditional style of mediumship.

If you are called to experiment with trance channeling I would suggest you work with a very experienced or trained medium who can guide you through the process.

If you don't have a coach you can try to communicate with one of your guides through the form of automatic writing.

Automatic writing is similar to trance however you are in a slightly-altered state and the spirit uses your hand to communicate a message by impressing into your mind a stream of thoughts, words and or a story.

The next time you meditate invite your guides to join you and send you a message. Make sure to have a pen and paper nearby and sit in a meditated state for at least 10-15 minutes before writing.

As you work with them, you may feel your hand tingle or sensations of the spirit world preparing to work with you. Ask them to give you a message or feel free to ask questions about them.

For example, What is their name? What are they helping you with right now? What is your highest purpose or mission? Notice what words pop into mind and just trust the process. No message is too cliché.

You can practice automatic writing also when you feel inspired such as inspirational writing. The message may sound more inspirational than esoteric but that is okay. The importance of it is to work on building the connection with spirit and allowing the messages to flow through you without interfering.

You want to be a clear channel always for the spirit world in any type of mediumship work you do.

Chapter 18: The Afterlife

When our loved ones transition to the afterlife, one of the biggest questions many of us ask are if they are okay. Working as a medium many people will ask you what the afterlife is like for our spirit loved ones and what happens when we cross over.

As our spirit loved ones transition their loved ones immediately come to greet them and guide them in their journey on the other side. They will reunite with friends, family, pets and spouses. Many spirits I have spoken to have told me they do not suffer at all and are restored to their full health, mental and physical.

They no longer have their earthly bodies but enter into a etheric body made of energy and thought. They often enter the tunnel of white light and connect with spiritual and heavenly beings as well which is why there are often stories told of meeting with saints, God or a religious figure.

In the afterlife, our spirit loved ones will have a life review where they meet with a guide or close relative who will guide them through a process of witnessing how they were on Earth, what lessons they learned and how they treated people. It isn't a painful experience but rather a witnessing of how you lived, what you did well and what you still need to work on.

They will learn what karmic relationships need to be healed and how to also move forward in their journeys on the other side.

Sometimes they stick around for their family to support them while they grieve and start over. Sometimes they try to heal relationships that went wrong or resolve unfinished business or conflict.

Other times Spirit has told me they continue their journey in evolving to the next stage or level in their spiritual purpose and may learn how to help people on the Earth plane or in the spirit world.

They may become a teacher, guide or continue the work they started on the Earth Plane on the other side.

Depending on how traumatic their life on Earth was they may also go through a period of recovery, healing and rehabilitation.

However one of the messages I hear most strongly from them is that they are never suffering. Each Spirit has a different purpose and journey on the other side just like we do here on Earth.

There are schools, communities and dimensions dedicated to learning different philosophies and helping one another in the process.

I like to think of it as spirit neighborhoods where they connect based on their similar path, interest or karmic lesson. They will experience real love, happiness and joy. They will change and evolve no matter how difficult or mean they may have been alive.

The afterlife is a continuation of their journey started on Earth and there are lessons that will continue to be learned and worked through for them and for us.

As they heal, they will also heal the family spiritual karma. Our spirit loved ones never want to see us grieve and suffer for too long.

They will send us signs, helpers and people to help us along our way as we also move forward through life without them.

As you develop your mediumship, practice also asking Spirit what the other side is like and how life continues.

You will be amazed at the response. It is truly an honor to work with Spirit and have access to such sacred information.

Chapter 19: Messages

One of the most powerful and impacting things about mediumship are the messages Spirit people want to give to their loved ones still alive. Imagine the feeling of not having the chance to say goodbye to someone who passed tragically and finally hearing a message from them in Spirit.

Mediums help to bring forth a lot of healing and transformation not only for the Spirit communicating but for the person receiving the message. In my work I am always humbled and awed by some of the messages Spirit gives to me to share with their loved one. The responses and feedback are life-changing and phenomenal.

You may feel the call to be a medium or perhaps you just want to practice and try to develop a closer relationship with a passed loved one. Either way, the experience can really provide a lot of wisdom and insight into what happens in the afterlife and where we go when we die.

I wasn't one to always give a lot of thought to the afterlife or where our souls go but through my spiritual development I discovered a whole new world that exists very much besides ours.

Our spirit loved ones are always there trying to influence us and show us signs, symbols and messages to catch our attention to let us know they never left.

When you work with Spirit and practice evidential mediumship it is always important to know what does the Spirit want to say to their loved one?

You can be a light worker and change the lives of so many people. You can help them on their path to healing and finding closure in their grief. Wherever mediumship or your spiritual path takes you there is no right or wrong road to go down as long as you are coming from a place of light and positive intention.

I always say "You don't choose Spirit, Spirit chooses you." For whatever reason, the Spirit person chose you to be the perfect instrument of communication to their loved one and will try their best to give you the information you need to help that person.

Some key things to remember in your practice of mediumship and spiritual development:

1. **Timing**- Everything in life is all about timing. Don't be frustrated if your mediumship isn't perfect right away. I guarantee you it never gets perfect but it will improve. With timing you will become much better with connecting to the Spirit World, giving great evidence and messages from the afterlife.

2. **Patience**- Patience is going to be your friend in any type of skill you are developing. Mediumship is similar to any other type of skill. You must practice and be willing to show up for the Spirit World and they will work with you as long as you are open and patient. Remember they want to get it right as much as you do.
3. **Compassion**- As you continue on your spiritual journey remember to have compassion for yourself, for the Spirit World and for anyone you work with. We are all fighting our own battles. Focus on healing yours and releasing any blockages that may be preventing you from having a deeper spiritual practice and connection to the Spirit World.
Don't be afraid to trust your intuition and higher self. It will lead you to new discoveries and deeper realms of truth and wisdom. Here you will find what you have been looking for and here you will connect with the highest source of all, love. Your Spirit loved ones are guiding you every step of the way.

"We are each gifted in a unique and important way. It is our privilege and our adventure to discover our own special light." – Mary Dunbar

Additional Mediumship Exercises

Spirit Poker Card Exercise

This exercise is great to practice with a friend. Each of you holds a poker card in your hand without telling each other what the card is. Now get into your meditative state and ask Spirit in your mind to show you what your partner's card is. Notice if you get the color (red/black) and the suit.

You may feel a presence around you. It may be a guide of yours or a passed loved one. If you don't feel anyone at all, it's okay. You can practice this exercise as many times as you want until you begin to feel the presence of Spirit around.

Spirit Photograph Exercise

You can practice this exercise with a friend or family member. Ask them to show you a photograph of a deceased loved one, preferably someone you didn't know that well or at all.

Take a look at photo and feel free to place your hand over it to draw in energy. Go into a meditative state and begin to connect with Spirit source. Once you feel a connection build, see if you can connect with the person in the photo.

You can ask in your mind for that person to make themselves aware to you. Notice any spirit impressions that come to mind or sensations. Ask the person questions about their life and how they passed. Now share with your partner and feel free to switch.

You can practice this exercise with anyone you don't much history about regarding deceased loved ones or relatives.

Letters to Your Spirit Loved One Exercise: This is a wonderful exercise and can bring forth a lot of healing for anyone who is grieving the loss of a loved one.

As in previous exercises, take a moment to get into a quiet meditative state. Make sure the environment is calm and quiet. Feel free to light a candle, burn incense or play soft music. Once you feel grounded and ready to communicate with Spirit move your awareness to your Spirit Loved Ones and concentrate on anyone that you would like to communicate with.

Concentrate on what you would say to your loved one if he/she was still there sitting in the room with you. When you are ready take a pen/paper and begin to write a letter to this person. Send the thought out to him/her that you'd like a response or sign that he/she received the letter. Now seal it and return back to it at the end of the week. Notice any impressions or feelings you received while writing the letter. Did you feel him/her around you or anyone from the Spirit World? When you return back to your letter, reflect on any messages or signs you think or felt were a response from Spirit.

Signs & Symbols from Spirit Exercise

Every morning before you start your day, take 5-10 minutes to reflect on what you are grateful for and visualize how your day will go. Feel free to send a thought out to the Spirit World and ask them to influence and guide you throughout your day. Ask for any repeating signs, symbols or images to pop out at you to let you know they are around. You can even ask for a specific passed loved one to give you a message or sign they are around during the day.

Spirit Dream Exercise

Before you go to bed at night close your day with some quiet time. Ask your Spirit Loved Ones to come visit you in your dreams or give you guidance in your sleep state. Also repeat the affirmation "When I wake up tomorrow I will remember all of my dreams." Concentrate on this affirmation and really believe you will remember all of your dreams.

When you wake up see if you remember any dreams from the night before. If not, keep practicing. Sometimes it takes a while to train our subconscious mind to remember. You can also download dream meditations for sleep or Spirit Guide meditations to listen to before you fall asleep. Happy Dreaming!

About Emily

Emily Stroia is a professional Intuitive and Medium based in the New York City metro and New Jersey area. She uses her intuition and mediumship abilities to offer guidance to all her clients, encouraging them to move forward in a positive direction no matter what obstacles the future has in store for them. She also updates a personal blog and teaches classes on developing your intuitive and spiritual gifts.

Currently, Emily lives in the greater NYC area and offers psychic readings by appointment only via in Person, Skype or Phone. To learn more about Emily, visit www.emilystroia.com

Other Books by Emily Stroia

Psychic Development for Beginners: A Practical Guide to Developing Your Intuition & Psychic Gifts

Free Downloads

Visit Emily's website to sign up for a free meditation.

Ready to Learn More?

Visit the intuitivesoulschool.com to sign up for Emily's spiritual development classes!

Printed in Dunstable, United Kingdom